ABANDONED
NEW MEXICO
ENIGMAS AND ENDINGS

SUSAN TATTERSON

AMERICA
THROUGH TIME®
ADDING COLOR TO AMERICAN HISTORY

For my wonderful Mum, Wendie, and my adventurous little sister, Nicole; for putting up with me living on the other side of the world. And for Heather Moulton—for the stop signs and so, so much more—you're the best sidekick ever!

America Through Time is an imprint of Fonthill Media LLC
www.through-time.com
office@through-time.com

Published by Arcadia Publishing by arrangement with Fonthill Media LLC
For all general information, please contact Arcadia Publishing:
Telephone: 843-853-2070
Fax: 843-853-0044
E-mail: sales@arcadiapublishing.com
For customer service and orders:
Toll-Free 1-888-313-2665

www.arcadiapublishing.com

First published 2019

Copyright © Susan Tatterson 2019

ISBN 978-1-63499-184-1

Typeset in Trade Gothic 10pt on 15pt
Printed and bound in England

CONTENTS

PREFACE

New Mexico's azure blue skies and iron red cliffs are as colorful as both its ancient and modern history. Under those enticing blue skies have lived ancient cultures, legendary cowboys, infamous warriors, and brave homesteaders settling the west, as well as soldiers from a plethora of armies. Claiming the oldest and highest, at 7,000 feet, capital city in the United States, Santa Fe was founded in 1610 and today hosts a flourishing artists' community and enchanting history. Established a little less than a century later by Spanish explorers, Albuquerque is the state's largest city and is an integral part of modern America's railroad history.

The state's ghost towns are captivating and plentiful but so too are some of its industrial and military remains. *Abandoned New Mexico: Enigmas and Endings* is a journey through not only some of New Mexico's especially colorful ghost towns like Shakespeare, but through industrial giants like the Albuquerque Rail Yards.

Trips through the southern and northern areas of the state, as well as everywhere in between, take the adventurous road tripper on a magical jaunt through history—you can sense the triumphs and struggles of the early settlers pushing ever further westward, leaving in their wake their temporary railroad and mining towns.

There is no shortage of abandoned military history in a state key to not only the protection of early settlers, but to the country during the Cold War era. In the north, during the 1950s, the Tierra Amarilla Air Force Station kept a watchful eye over the Los Alamos National Laboratory. While almost a century earlier in the south, Fort Bayard's famous Buffalo Soldiers guarded the pioneering families looking to make New Mexico their home.

As with other states I have explored and photographed, New Mexico's abandonments share much with their counterparts—without human intervention they take on a life of their own and now possess a mythical quality. They tell their stories with light, color and decay. They inspire us to imagine what went on within their walls and on their streets, and they have led me on a wondrous and thought-provoking journey into America's past.

In 1941, New Mexico license plates began displaying "Land of Enchantment"; in 1999, this tagline became the official nickname of the state. In my extensive travels of the state, I cannot deny the truth in these words; it is in fact enchanting, but it is also home to some of the most genuinely helpful people with a passion for their history that I have had the good fortune to meet, and without whom, many of the photos in this book would simply not exist. It will be impossible to thank all of them here, but I will do my best.

A huge thank you to all involved in my efforts to capture the iconic Albuquerque Rail Yards: Leba Freed, president of the Wheels Museum, who went above and beyond to show me around her museum and the area of the Yards she had access to. She went a step further though and contacted the City of Albuquerque and pushed for me to be given permission to photograph the unforgettable machine shop and the other abandoned buildings on the massive site. Gabe Rivera, Development Coordinator, who kindly gave of his time to unlock the gates of the Yards for me and who left me to explore a photographer's "abandoned paradise." Doyle Caton, a true gentleman and wonderful historian with extensive knowledge of the Santa Fe Railroad and the Rail Yards—you are a treasure!

Many of New Mexico's ghost towns are on private land and I have their owners to thank for the unlimited access I was granted. Dave and Regina Ochsenbine, the brave couple who are embarking on an adventure of a lifetime to keep their recently acquired town of Shakespeare alive. The history of this town is inspiring, and I am incredibly grateful for the opportunity to photograph it. Melissa Lamoree, for allowing me to spend hours documenting Steins, the railroad ghost town she is opening for tours in honor of the memory of her grandfather, Larry Link, who was brutally murdered there in 2011.

And last but certainly not least, Rocky Hildebrand, caretaker and passionate advocate for Fort Bayard, who spent many hours opening the Fort's buildings for me and enlightening me to the importance of its history—your knowledge was invaluable but it is your sense of humor I will always remember—thank you!

I know there are many more acknowledgements due, but I am out of space, and off to my next New Mexico adventure! I hope these photographs inspire your curiosity as much as the places have mine. Keep adventuring!

Sue Tatterson
Gold Canyon, 2019

ALBUQUERQUE RAIL YARDS

Steam locomotives were the heartbeat of the settlement of America and the backbone of industrial growth; similarly, Albuquerque's Rail Yards became the heartbeat of an emerging city. Today, walking through the yard's machine shop, it is hard not to be struck by the reverberating silence echoing through the once bustling facility. The silence holds not only the memories of what was, but the promise of what can be. The 165,000-square-foot broken steel and glass shell is the embodiment of this hushed promise. This massive empty building, the largest of the Rail Yard's remaining structures, which once vibrated with the energy and passions of a country at war, now stands eerily mute, awaiting its next chapter.

Historians credit the railroad as an integral part of Albuquerque's development. As the rush to settle the west pushed forward, the Santa Fe railway became the city's largest employer. In 1919, the locomotive shops employed almost 1,000 workers, which at the time was a quarter of the city's workforce. A lumber yard, foundry, mill, and other businesses associated with the railroad became established and most of Albuquerque's residents relied on the railroad for their livelihood.

Many of the buildings that comprise the 27-acre complex were built between 1914 and 1924 by the Atchison, Topeka & Santa Fe Railway. Their counterparts, built as early as 1880, including the historically significant roundhouse, have sadly been demolished. The machine shop opened in 1921, after being erected in only eight months; it stands as a tribute to the beginning era of industrial design and was once compared to the revolutionary Ford River Rouge Glass Plant. The striking steel frame building, with almost 60-foot-high walls of glass panels, operated at its peak in the 1940s and stood as an icon to innovation and expansion. Designed to

The machine shop has often been nicknamed "The Cathedral."

allow maximum light exposure the building operated twenty-four hours a day during World War II, and at its zenith, during the war years, employed 1,500 workers.

After the war, steam locomotives were made obsolete by the more efficient diesel engines, as they were more cost effective to operate and could run longer without servicing. And so began the slow demise of the Albuquerque Rail Yards and its shops. Without the constant need for servicing and overhauls required by steam locomotives, the workforce at the yards slowly dwindled and, by the 1950s, was operating with only 200 employees and the shops became used for rail line maintenance.

Second chances are few for obsolesced technology; chances are often nonexistent for the locations that were its lifeblood. The Rail Yards were officially closed in the 1990s and were purchased by the City of Albuquerque in 2007. As is the case with so many redevelopment plans in America's cities, the plans for mixed reuse of the Rail Yards stopped and started several times, but now in 2019, it looks set to finally move forward. Anchoring this move forward is the WHEELS museum, occupying 21,000 square feet of what was once the storehouse, the museum is a delight to explore and the number of historical artifacts it has on display is remarkable. Its passionate staff, all volunteers, work tirelessly to promote the next phase in the Rail Yards' history.

Diesel, "Netflixed"(the newly coined term used to describe the demise of a company or technology by a more efficient competitor) steam. Ironically, Netflix, may in fact be the savior of the Albuquerque Rail Yards. In 2018, Netflix purchased the ABQ Studios, and with plans to invest $1 billion over the next ten years and create more than 1,000 jobs, many are touting New Mexico's largest city as the "new Hollywood." The purchase led to the signing of an agreement, in early 2019, between the City of Albuquerque and Central New Mexico Community College to bring the College's Film Production Center of Excellence to the Rail Yards. If the partnership proceeds, Central New Mexico Community College will be the Rail Yard's first tenant in more than twenty years.

The Albuquerque Rail Yards are no stranger to life reimagined as a movie set, and have been the location for scenes in *Avengers* as well as many other popular TV series and movies. Only time will tell if the opportunity for the yards to once again become a thriving part of the city, and the backbone of a new industry, eventuates.

A long-abandoned workstation.

A colorful fire hose reel stands apart from heavily grime-covered windows.

A rusted out hook on the machine shop floor.

Tracks inside the machine shop leading to the transfer table.

Wood flooring blocks in the machine shop.

Above: A wall of hundeds of glass panes surrounds the steel frame of the machine shop.

Opposite page: Afternoon sunlight streams through an open door of the machine shop.

The transfer table strewn with weeds.

One of the massive cranes built into the ceiling of the machine shop.

A burnt-out area of the boiler shop.

The transfer table.

The rusted transfer table platform.

Most of the glass panes at rooftop level have been destroyed.

The exterior of the Blacksmith shop.

The exterior of the locker rooms, some of the smaller outer structures will not be part of the revitalization.

Above: The underside of an overhead crane.

Opposite page: The overhead travelling cranes were integrated into the building's structure.

The view across the transfer table to the machine shop.

The steel frame and glass panes allowed for maximum natural light to enter the building.

The sandstone exterior of the fire station, it was built in 1920.

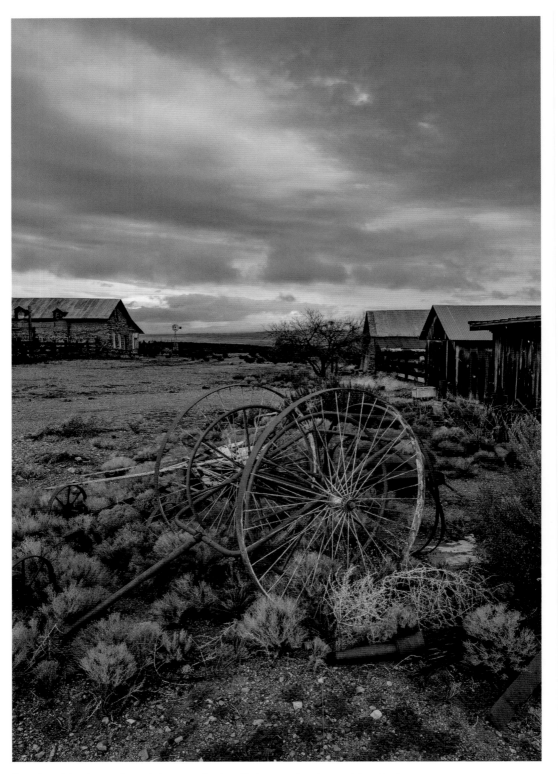

Remains of the day—a discarded wagon wheel on Shakespeare's only remaining street.

SHAKESPEARE

A diamond swindle, more name changes than a chameleon changing its colors, and a tale of two strong, courageous women set the scene for a drama worthy of a Shakespearian play. The town of Shakespeare shares not only its name with the famous English playwright, but its main street is aptly called Avon Avenue and its one hotel bears the name Stratford. While the irony cannot be denied, could there have been an unintentional forewarning of the tragedies and farces that would play out on the streets of this dusty, wild, lawless mining town of the Southwest?

Shakespeare and its colorful history exist today because of the passion Rita Hill and her daughter, Janaloo, shared for the town they called home, and for the power of familial bonds. The importance of shared history and the significance of collecting stories drove the two women to compile a detailed and comprehensive timeline of the settling and demise of the small town with a famous name.

The earth's precious minerals drew pioneers and prospectors westward, but a commodity even more precious—fresh water—drew travelers to Shakespeare, known then as Mexican Springs, and led to the town's settlement. According to Rita Hill's thoroughly researched history of the town, Mexican Spring's first permanent residents were settled around 1856 when regular mail service, associated with the Butterfield line, began through the area.

Both Confederate and Union soldiers spent time in Mexican Springs, but it was not until after the war that the town became known as Grant. In 1865, John Evensen, a Norwegian native, arrived in Mexican Springs and was hired as a station-keeper, he soon changed the name of the town in honor of the Union General. The name change would not last long as the mining boom would soon begin.

A California financier, William Ralston, can be credited with the silver rush that put Grant on the map and saw the town boom, change its name to Ralston City—and bust. The silver ore was neither abundant nor of a high quality and the mines soon closed. At this point in Shakespeare's history, the plot detours from that of a typical boom, bust mining town to the location of one of the biggest diamond swindles in the history of the Southwest.

Reportedly, the area around Lee's Peak was salted with diamonds and the Texas boys—men hired to protect the company's silver mine interests—flashed a cigar box full of rough diamonds around Shakespeare, claiming they found them while mining the area around Mt. Aera, which is today known as Lee's Peak. No exact location of the diamond field was ever officially reported, but William Ralston's involvement in the ensuing diamond company deal led to rumors that Ralston City must be the location. The possibility of extreme wealth fired imaginations and a frenzy of prospectors swelled the population of the almost ghost town to more than 3000; and so began Shakespeare's second boom.

The diamond boom ended abruptly when a diamond, bearing the marks of a cutting wheel, was found and the hoax was revealed. Stories vary on the specifics surrounding how the swindle was brought down and the aftermath, many say Ralston's business partner left the country—with the money he had made in stocks—and left Ralston to account for the losses. Ralston died from apparent suicide when his banking empire collapsed in 1875; the business collapse is not attributed to the diamond heist, although Shakespeare stories propose otherwise.

Ralston City was once again deserted and became the home of ranchers, some die-hard miners and several business owners who remained to provide goods and services, as well as John Evensen the station-keeper. In the late 1870s, Col. William Boyle and Gen. John Boyle formed the Shakespeare Gold and Silver Mining Company and filed many of the old Ralston claims and once again started mining. They renamed Ralston City, to Shakespeare; Main Street became Avon Avenue, and they established the Stratford Hotel.

Throughout the decades that followed, legends were born, and history made and remade into the stories that have become Shakespeare's lore. Billy the Kid washed dishes at the Stratford and Arizona's future governor, George P. Hunt, waited tables. Tales of hangings and shootings, and bodies carried through the darkness and dumped across the rail line to disguise the cause of death, abound. Two characters, Sandy King and Russian Bill, were hanged from a rafter in Grant House. King for being a "damned nuisance" and Russian Bill for horse theft. Their bodies hanged in the dining room of Grant House overnight, and the story goes that when the stagecoach passengers arrived for breakfast the next morning, they were greeted by the two men's bodies.

Grant House, where Sandy King and Russian Bill were hanged as well as many others.

The mail station, the oldest building in Shakespeare.

Avon Avenue at sunset.

The tales of the goings-on in Shakespeare, up until the Depression hit in 1932, could fill volumes. The mines in the area closed and almost instantly the residents and miners moved on and Shakespeare's life as a town ceased. The death and drama that had played out on its streets and within the walls of its saloons, hotels, and homes left behind only ghosts.

It was not until 1935, when Frank and Rita Hill purchased the property for ranching, that its next and continuing act would begin. As fate would have it, their indomitable spirits would keep Shakespeare alive well into the next century. The Hills made their home in the old mercantile building and restored and maintained many of the failing adobe structures while managing the everyday operations of the ranch. They lived without electricity and running water, and their daughter, Janaloo, was raised without what we consider necessities.

The stories of the Hill family, especially the women, are as legendary as the town itself. Rita's feisty, do not-mess-with-me character led to her being dragged off to jail for what became known locally as "The Great Highway Fight." In 1973, a few years after Frank's death, Rita and Janaloo were managing the ranch and Shakespeare alone—a daunting task at best. They were approached by the State Highway Department and advised that they would be taking almost 60 acres of their land as well as the State Trust Land they leased. A battle ensued, both in court and on the Hill's property. Rita staged a protest, a sit-in, in an 8-foot-square wooden shack. A makeshift bed was set up for the seventy-one-year-old Rita, and Janaloo would bring her food and water daily. The protest lasted through the brutal summer months of August and September and finally ended on November 23, with Rita being hauled off to prison for seventeen days. In true Shakespearian fashion, Janaloo recalled in her book, *The Hill Family of Shakespeare*, the fight swung "back and forth between comedy and tragedy."

Rita died in 1985, just before her eighty-fourth birthday. Janaloo, continued her mother's legacy, writing several books on the history of Shakespeare and the Hill Family. She and her husband, Manny Hough, continued to work the ranch as well as maintain and promote their ghost town. Through sheer tenacity, by the mid-1990s, they increased the number of annual visitors to 5,000.

In 1995, after adding much-needed roofing to the town's many original adobe buildings, Manny convinced Janaloo to invest in improvements to the Mercantile— their home. Several years earlier, they ran electricity to the property, and they fulfilled one of Rita and Janaloo's dreams of converting the Mercantile basement into an apartment. You can feel the excitement and pleasure in Janaloo's words as she describes, in her book, the new renovation and how she loved to be able to walk up the stairs from the basement apartment to all "the old things" she loved. She spoke of family heirlooms and described irreplaceable antiques from Shakespeare's early days.

Heartbreakingly, in 1997, tragedy struck only a few months after the renovations were complete. A fire, fueled by 50 mile per hour winds, devastated the Mercantile. Janaloo and Manny lost everything. Manny suffered second- and third-degree burns and Janaloo suffered smoke inhalation from trying to save the precious history she had spent her life preserving—all but a few draws of research were lost. The town and friends from far and wide started a fund and soon a new home was being built, one where Janaloo would spend her remaining years. Not long before the home was completed, she was diagnosed with an aggressive form of cancer. Janaloo passed away in 2005, after, true to character, putting up a heroic fight, leaving her beloved ghost town Shakespeare to her other true love, Manny, to run.

Manny honored Janaloo's memory and continued to maintain the town and show visitors through as often as he could. He continued to live in Shakespeare until his death in 2018. Just when it appeared Shakespeare's final act was looming, Manny's daughter, Regina, from a previous marriage, and her husband, Dave, packed up their life in the Midwest and settled in Shakespeare. Sharing the same grit and determination the Hill's possessed, they have embarked on the task of keeping Shakespeare alive, and with Frank, Rita, Janaloo, and Manny watching over them from their graves atop the hill at the end of Avon Avenue, they just may have a fighting chance.

Above: The remains of a wagon train with The Stratford Hotel in the background.

Opposite page: Looking out from the mail station window.

The Stratford Hotel.

Personal items in the downstairs front room of the Stratford Hotel.

An original bedframe stands in a downstairs bedroom of the Stratford Hotel.

The dining room of the Stratford, where Arizona Governor-to-be George P. Hunt waited tables.

An upstairs room in the Stratford.

The Stratford's rooms contained the barest of necessities and visitors often shared rooms with strangers.

The large kitchen area of Grant House, run by station-keeper John Evensen.

The saloon at Grant House.

Miner's hats and whiskey bottles in the Grant House saloon.

The assay office.

Tools of the trade inside the assay office.

The blacksmith building filled with tools.

The tools used to repair wagon wheels sit bathed in sunlight, gathering spider webs.

The tiny building where Rita Hill staged her protest against the Highway Administration. She lived in this tiny space for many months.

Looking down over their town, the gravesites of the Hill family at the top of Avon Avenue

TIERRA AMARILLA AIRFORCE STATION

Reminiscent of the secretive Cold War era it was built during, the Tierra Amarilla Airforce Station is best described as hidden. The station is located along an isolated northern New Mexico Road and the remains of the almost unnoticeable entrance give scant indication of what remains on the grounds. Nor do the trashed buildings give any indication of the importance of the military installation that once served the country during the 1950s.

The initial 80 acres of land for the base were purchased from ranchers in 1949, with The Department of Defense eventually amassing 107 acres for the military site. At a peak elevation of 7,301 feet, the top of the mesa, which was flattened even further during site development, offers spectacular views stretching more than 60 miles to the east, south, and west and is an ideal location for a radar site. Tierra Amarilla Airforce Station, or El Vado Radar Site, as it was also sometimes called, acted as an aircraft control and warning station and provided coverage for the Los Alamos National Laboratory. According to records, in March 1952, almost 7,000 aircraft were plotted at distances of up to 140 miles—the skies above the station kept the 767th AC&W Squadron busy.

Cold War radar sites, throughout the world, were not built to win architectural awards; they were serviceable at best and barren at worst, and while Tierra Amarilla was no exception with its concrete block buildings and utilitarian site plan, the stunning southwest landscape set it apart from most others.

December 1958 saw the closure of the base—its lifespan short but successful. The site was used briefly in the early 1960s by the Forestry and Resource Conservation Division but was soon turned over to the Northern New Mexico Community College District. Since then the site has remained abandoned, although in 2001 it was registered with the National Register of Historic Places and a comprehensive reuse study was completed in 2003. The study yielded no tangible results and more than a decade later, the base continues to disintegrate into itself.

Communication Receiver building.

The Operations building.

The garage attached to the Operations building.

Modern day ruins of the Cold War era.

A decaying dormitory.

A restricted area inside the Operations building.

An interior hallway of the Operations building.

Interior of the heating plant.

The rotting shell of the upstairs floor of a dormitory.

Above: The roofless and wall-less upstairs of a dormitory.

Opposite page: Sunset as seen through the broken steel door of the Communications Receiver building.

A puddle formed from melted snow reflects the side view of an Officer's Row residence.

FORT BAYARD

An air of expectation surrounds Fort Bayard's parade ground and its bordering Officer's Row residences. Their wide, welcoming, wrap-around porches beckon to be restored with porch swings and laughter. Instead, the stark silence that greets visitors seems out of place; the street with the extended sidewalks and mansions should be filled with people and it vibrates with an energy that wants to be filled with people—it is not a ghostly feeling, but it is an uncomfortable one. There seems to be unfinished business at Fort Bayard, and if you ask the volunteers who run the historical society and care for the grounds, they are certain there is.

The Fort, made famous by the Buffalo Soldiers and established in 1866 to offer protection to the early settlers of the area from the Warm Springs Apache, was also used in the campaign to capture Geronimo. Its military role evolved and when it closed as a fort in 1899, the next century saw it become the first sanatorium dedicated to the treatment of army personnel suffering from tuberculosis. It would continue to be used as a medical facility in a variety of capacities for more than 100 years. It closed permanently in 2010 due to the deteriorating state of its buildings.

Preservationists fought for many years to keep the main hospital building from being demolished; while they were not successful at preserving the hospital, they are continuing to argue for the redevelopment of the Fort Bayard Site. There is a push to have the site turned over to Grant County and the Fort Bayard Historic Preservation Society; in the hands of these passionate locals, Fort Bayard's parade ground and tree-lined streets may yet play host to celebrations of its cultural history.

Above: Officer's Row residences line the parade ground at Fort Bayard.

Opposite page: A deteriorating exterior of an Officer's Row residence.

A home overgrown with grass and weeds.

A weathered front porch of a married employees cottage.

Fort Bayard's streets are filled with empty decaying residences.

A barren landscape surrounds this former employee residence.

The entrance hall of an Officer's Row residence. The mansions were divided into apartments.

A garishly painted kitchen.

A bathroom in need of renovations.

The rear access road to the Officer's Row residences.

The nurses' quarters.

The decommisioned Fort Bayard Fire Truck.

The interior of the 1955 International Fire Truck.

STEINS

I t appears written into Southwest ghost town lore: there will be a history of violent deaths, either by hanging or shooting or other unfortunate means. Surprisingly we expect and are not shocked by the tales of violence that plagued these lawless towns. Steins ghost town lives up to this reputation, but tragically it is a modern-day, unsolved murder that haunts its dusty streets and continues to break the hearts of the Link family who have owned the town since 1988.

Larry Link was shot five times in cold blood with an untraceable gun in the early morning hours of June 7, 2011, a few feet outside the fenced perimeter of the ghost town he and his family had worked hard to restore. The murder remains unsolved and speculation abounds. Steins became closed to visitors after the murder but Link's granddaughter, Melissa, has resolutely reopened the town to visitors and provides tours as often as her busy schedule allows.

Steins was settled in 1880 as a Southern Pacific Railroad town, and in the early 1900s, a quarry was established in the surrounding rocky slopes to produce crushed rock for the railroad bed. Named after Captain Enoch Steens, a military officer who left behind a legacy of western exploration and honorable service to the United States, the town had a shorter lifespan than its namesake. The quarry closed in 1925 and the slow demise of the town continued until the end of World War II. The railroad ceased using Steins as a stop, which meant the residents no longer received subsidized water from the railroad; as a town without its own water supply this signaled the end of the road. The Southern Pacific offered the town's remaining residents free transportation to any other railroad town of their choice; taking only the possessions they could carry Steins' residents took up the offer and moved on.

In 1964, a fire tore through the abandoned town destroying many of its remaining buildings. The Link family faithfully restored much of the town and it stands today as a time-capsule to the harshness of life in a town that legend says was built on rock so hard and dry the graves in the nearby cemetery had to be blasted and not dug. Steins' future is perhaps brighter than when it was forsaken in the 1940s but its continued existence is precarious at best and dependent on the passion of a young woman, whose childhood memories and love for her grandfather's memory inspire her to share her family's ghost town with curious travelers.

The Steins Mercantile.

Spider web encrusted and tattered clothing lays on a dusty bed.

A cornucopia of relics fills a room in one of the abandoned homes.

Afternoon sunlight streams into a disused kitchen.

A giant iron pot once used to boil water to wash clothes.

The remains of a wagon train.

A wagon wheel in need of repair surrounded by blacksmithing tools.

Collectibles from the town's heyday fill both the inside and outside of the buildings.

Narrow pathways lead between the adobe homes of Steins.

A windmill blade attached to a rusted shed wall.

A water supply truck.

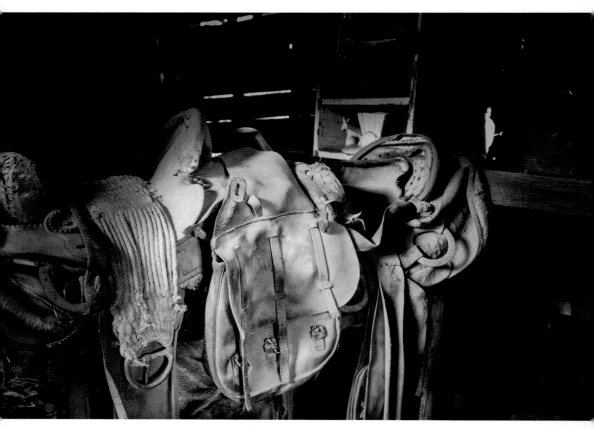

Above: An aging saddle and saddlebags gathering dust.

Opposite page: Well-worn boots hang from a beam.

An antique typewriter smothered in cobwebs.

A poster celebrating the opening of a Union Pacific rail route.

The sun sets on discarded farming equipment and a decaying stagecoach.

A barely standing fence surrounds a Steins home.

The rotting wooden frame of a long-abandoned stagecoach.

Discarded mining equipment overshadows the view across the valley towards Monument Peak.

LAKE VALLEY

Blacksmith John Leavitt may well have felt like he was Aladdin walking into the Cave of Wonders when, in 1881, he found himself surrounded by shimmering walls of silver. Leavitt, after only two days of digging, uncovered a cavern that become known as the Bridal Chamber, and which is still considered the largest discovery of silver in the history of mining. The chamber measured 26 feet across and 12 feet high and held silver ore so pure it was shipped unsmelted to the mint. And so began the rise and quick-to-follow fall of Lake Valley, another mining town with great riches and a short existence.

In 1878, Lake Valley provided early prospectors, George Lufkin and Chris Watson, with silver samples considered valuable enough for a syndicate, headed by George Daly, to buy all the claims in the area for a reported $225,000. Legend tells us Leavitt's claim, where the Bridal Chamber was found, had been dug a few feet by Lufkin and Watson when they first explored the area, but they had not continued that extra few feet to the glittering fortune that lay so near. In a cruel twist of fate, the day Leavitt discovered the cavern, which ultimately gave out almost 2.5 million ounces of silver, Daly was murdered by the Apaches.

Lake Valley died swiftly with the silver panic of 1893, and in 1895, the then mostly quiet Main Street caught fire and burned to the ground. For the next century, it remained home to a few miners and residents, but in 1994, the town's last remaining stalwarts left. Today, the crumbling remains of the town are managed by the BLM. The old schoolhouse has been restored and operates as a museum.

The Lake Valley gas station.

The schoolhouse, which has been renovated and acts as a museum.

The church, as seen through what remains of a stone building on Main Street.

Time and the elements are taking a toll on what remains of Lake Valley's buildings.

The wide Main Street is lined with crumbling residences.

Lake Valley ruins with Monument Peak far off in the distance.

Above: Water tanks at the top of the hill overlooking the town.

Opposite page: An old crate that once carried grease.

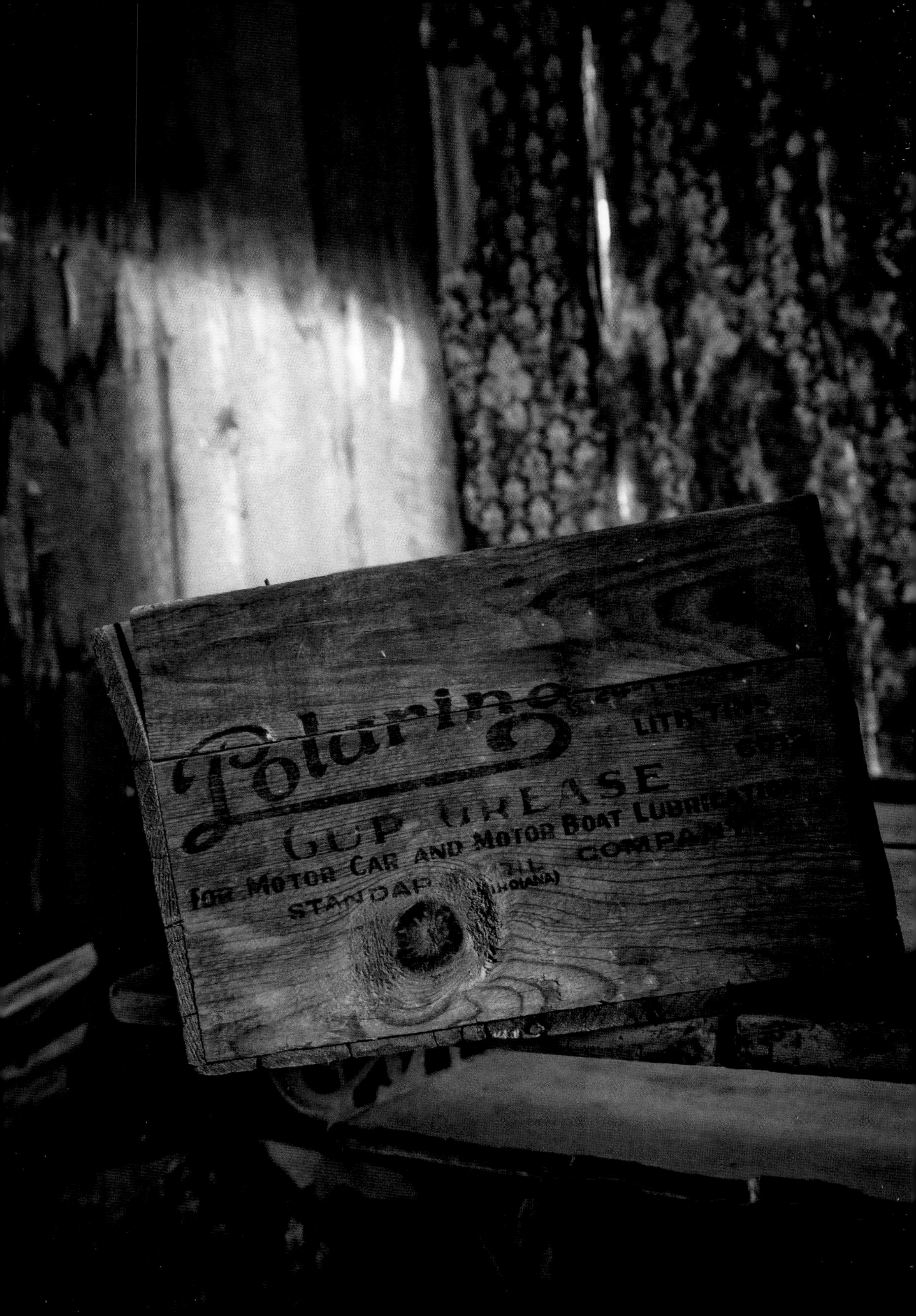
Polarine
CUP GREASE
FOR MOTOR CAR AND MOTOR BOAT

What remains of Nowlin House, where one of Lake Valley's longest residents, Blanche Nowlin, lived.

Muddy fingerprints on a dirty covered window add a human touch to an otherwise deserted town.

Only an outer wall remains of this stone house.

A building associated with the mine has breathtaking views across the valley to Monument Peak.

Discarded mining equipment.

Nature trying to reclaim the land from what remains of Lake Valley's mining days.

What remains of the Cedarvale school.

The roof has collaped in on the northeast side of the school.

CEDARVALE

L and exhausted by man's unforgiving farming practices has a sense of desolation even more profound than the remains of the buildings we leave surrounding it. There is a poetic loneliness in abandoned farmland. Cedarvale is nothing more than a hiccup in New Mexico's history; all that remains of its short-lived farming days are a wasteland of weed infested, overgrown earth and dirt that once generously offered its nutrients to feed a growing country and those defending it.

Settled in 1908 alongside the New Mexico Central Railroad Route, Cedarvale was named after Cedar Vale in Kansas. Pioneering families, led by three Kansas men, Edward Smith, William Taylor, and Oliver P. DeWolfe, were drawn to central New Mexico by the promise a farm on homesteaded land. The star crop of the area was pinto beans, as they had a short growing season and could be dry farmed. There was a ready market in New Mexico and they were used to feed soldiers during World War I.

The town quickly grew, and in 1917, a bond was issued to erect a school on land adjacent to what is now Rt. 42. In 1935, the Depression-era Works Program Administration expanded the school to include four classrooms and a large gymnasium. The school, at its peak, served fifty students and was an integral part of the community, with the gym often used as a social gathering place. Today, the school is succumbing to neglect and isolation; the town's residents having long ago moved on. The Depression and drought forced the farming families to settle elsewhere; their former homes are now slowly being reclaimed by nature.

Above: Attached desk chairs in a decaying classroom.

Opposite page: The entry to the main corridor of Cedarvale's school

An old decaying farmhouse replete with warnings.

Looking out at stormy skies from inside one of Cedarvale's rotting homes.

A weathered farm shed.

A desolate abandoned farming-town scene.

Above: The Cedarvale school's gymnasium floor is covered in organic debris and tumbleweed.

Opposite page: The crumbling west facing wall of the gymnasium.

A twisted tree frames an old farmhouse.

An empty farmhouse sits on the barren plains of Cedarvale.

Wind and rain have lashed at this open door, destroying its panels.

A door-less, door frame frames the incoming storm.

A dilapidated structure overgrown with grass and weeds.

The front of the abandoned school is severely damaged by weather and vandals.

The east wall of the school showing the underlying brickwork and the collapsed roof.

Inside the school gymnasium, water damage is ongoing.

KELLY/KELLY MINE

Kelly Mine was once surrounded by a bustling town with a population of more than three thousand residents. In its heyday, the town of Kelly once boasted many businesses and organizations, including two hotels, two dance halls, two schools, and three churches: Catholic, Methodist, and Presbyterian, with the Catholic church now the only remaining structure in Kelly. Of the mine, all that remains are the head frame, tailing dumps, and the crumbling foundations of the smelter. The remains of the mine offer breathtaking views of the surrounding Magdalena Mountains.

In 1866, J. S. Hutchason discovered rich lead outcroppings and soon the mountains were providing miners with both lead and silver ore. The mining district founded by Hutchason flourished well into the latter part of the nineteenth century. The 1893 silver crash caused Kelly to struggle—but only momentarily; even more abundance lay buried in the mountains. In 1903, the discovery, by Cory T. Brown, of green rocks in the discard piles of the mine set the scene for Kelly's most successful decades. The "green rocks" were smithsonite, a form of zinc carbonate, and brought wealth and prosperity to the town.

By the 1930s, the smithsonite was all but depleted and Kelly went the way of all mining towns: when the mine's riches were stripped, it became a ghost town. For many years, Kelly's buildings stood empty and abandoned and suffered at the hands of vandals. Residents of nearby Magdalena slowly started removing the buildings and their materials and repurposing them. Today, no vestige of the town remains and, wandering through the ruins of the mine, it is almost impossible to imagine a bustling town once stood in the shadows of the towering head frame—its wooden trusses and dangling sheets of rusted cladding a stark reminder of how quickly we plunder the earth and then move on.

The mine's smelting furnace.

The collapsing wooden section of the mine's headframe.

Smelter foundations and furnace stacks.

The Kelly Mine steel headframe stands ominously against the sky.

Above: The Kelly headframe stands 121 feet above the entrance to the mineshaft.

Opposite page: The remains of the shaft entrance frame the smelter furnace and the Magdalena Mountains.

A southern-facing view of the smelter remains.

The smelter was built by the Tri-Bullion Mining and Smelting Company.

The mineshaft entrance stands above a 1,000-foot drop into the depths of the earth.

The view inside the smelter furnace tower looking skyward.

The shaft entrance leads to more then 30 miles of tunnels.

The Traylor Headframe was constructed on site by Gustav Billing.

Much of the top section of the shaft has fallen, what remains balances precariously.

Smelter foundation ruins on the way to Kelly.

Although modern, these smelter ruins have taken on an almost ancient appearance.

Above: The Magdalena Mountains act as a beautiful backdrop to these ruins, which are on the road to Kelly.

Opposite page: Smelter ruins belonging to a Kelly Mine neighbor.

BIBLIOGRAPHY

Albuquerque Rail Yards: Redeveloping the City's Historic Rail Yards (PDF) (Report). *Urban Land Institute*. February 2008. Retrieved March 1, 2019

Barnitz, Katy "City takes control of the Rail Yards." *Albuquerque Journal*. September 16, 2018. Retrieved March 2, 2019

Cherry/See Architects. "Re-use Study for Tierra Amarilla AFS P-8 Radar Site Historic District." New Mexico Historic Preservation Division, September 2003. Retrieved from https://www.radomes.org/museum/documents/Tierra20 Amarilla20reuse20study.pdf

Contreras, Russell. Ghost Town to Reopen as Murder Stays Unsolved. *Albuquerque Journal*. February 6, 2012 Retrieved March 29, 2019 from https://www.abqjournal.com/85647/ghost-town-to-reopen-as-murder-stays-unsolved.html

Hill, Janaloo. *The Hill Family of Shakespeare*. Shakespeare, New Mexico: Janaloo Hill, 2001

Hill, Rita. *Then and Now, Here and Around Shakespeare*. Lordsburg, New Mexico: Lordsburg Hidalgo County Chamber of Commerce, 1963

Hyatt, Robert. "The Great Diamond Hoax." *The Desert Magazine Volume 29, No. 11*. November 1966.

Kammer, David. Establishment of Fort Bayard Army Post. New Mexico History. Retrieved March 8, 2019 from https://newmexicohistory.org/places/fort-bayard

Montoya, Susan. NM's historic Fort Bayard up for sale. *Albuquerque Journal*. February 2, 2014. Retrieved March 7, 2019 from https://www.abqjournal.com/346485/nms-historic-fort-bayard-up-for-sale.html

Mulhouse, John. "No Rattlesnakes/No Pinto Beans: Cedarvale, NM." City of Dust, October 23, 2015. Retrieved March 15, 2019 from http://cityofdust.blogspot.com/2015/10/no-rattlesnakesno-pinto-beans-cedarvale.html

Mulhouse, John. "The Bridal Chamber: Lake Valley, New Mexico." City of Dust, July 16, 2015. Retrieved April 5, 2019 from http://cityofdust.blogspot.com/2015/07/the-bridal-chamber-lake-valley-new.html

Mulhouse, John. "Troubled Times: Steins, New Mexico." City of Dust, February, 2014. Retrieved March 23, 2019 from http://cityofdust.blogspot.com/2014/02/troubled-times-steins-new-mexico.html

Murbarger, Nell. "They Live in a Ghost Town." *The Desert Magazine Volume 12, No. 10*. August 1949.

National Register for Historic Places. National Register for Historic Places: Registration, Form Tierra Amarilla AFS P-8 Historic District. Retrieved from https://npgallery.nps.gov/GetAsset/5c0c549a-360e-420b-b4b8-55d4bf991861

Pike, David. *Roadside New Mexico, A Guide to Historic Markers*. Albuquerque, New Mexico: University of New Mexico Press, 2015.

Plant, Geoffrey. Preservation group backing plan for Fort Bayard. *Silver City Daily Press*. February 8, 2019 Retrieved March 5, 2019 from http://www.scdailypress.com/site/2019/02/08/preservation-group-backing-plan-for-fort-bayard/

Sherman, James E & Barbara H. *Ghost Towns and Mining Camps of New Mexico* . Norman, Oklahoma: University of Oklahoma Press, 1975

Varney, Phillip. *New Mexico's Best Ghost Towns*. Albuquerque, New Mexico: University of New Mexico Press, 1987.

Weiser, Kathy. "Steins, New Mexico - A Railroad Ghost Town." Legends of America, September, 2016. Retrieved March 22, 2019 from https://www.legendsofamerica.com/nm-steins/

Wilson, Chris. The Historic Railroad Buildings of Albuquerque: An Assessment of Significance. Retrieved March 5, 2019 from http://wheelsmuseum.org/wp-content/uploads/2015/11/The-Historic-Railroad-Buildings-of-Albuquerque.pdf.